Magi Gibson

TARANIS BOOKS

Design - Alan Mason

Printed in Scotland by Clydeside Press, Glasgow

ISBN 1-873899-65-3

Thanks to EM-DEE for additional typesetting

The publishers acknowledge the financial assistance of the
Scottish Arts Council in the publication of this volume

ACKNOWLEDGEMENTS

Some of these poems have appeared in the following publications:

Anthologies

Fresh Oceans (Stramullion)
I wouldn't thank you for a valentine (Viking)
Meantime (Polygon)
Original Prints 4 (Polygon)
Recurring Themes (W.E.A.)

Newspapers & Magazines

Cencrastus
Chapman
Gairfish
Harpies & Quines
Northlight
Northwords
Radical Scotland
Spectrum
West Coast Magazine

CONTENTS

for Jim

Under the silken sky of India

He holds her tiny body
with the awkwardness and tenderness
of the first-time father

A girl, his wife murmurs
tears in her eyes

Behind the house
under the shining moon
in the shelter of a banyan tree
he kisses his new-born daughter's lips
with opium, he stops her tiny nose
with dampened sand

Behind the house
under the dark shroud of the sky
he holds her lifeless body
with the awkwardness
of the first-time murderer
and weeps at the pain
he hoped he would not feel
and buries his guilt
in the shelter of the banyan tree

Never again can he look
into the eyes of his wife
without drowning in her tears

And when he says her name
and reaches out to touch her
he thinks how easy it would be
to kill her when she turns her head
and looks the other way

**Are eyes the windows of the soul
or mirrors on the world?**

The optometrist says my eyes are fine
With a telescope I see the stars
With binoculars I can transform a smudge
into a waving child. With a microscope
and my emotions on the agar plate
I can see what's bugging me. With
rose-coloured spectacles I can forget

I read his chart. I know it says

G
O B
B L D Y G
O O K G O B

B L D Y G O O K

G O B B L D Y G O O K

He puts some crazy glasses on my nose
I look into a small machine
A dot of light dances in the dark
I say we are all dots of light
A mad inventor keeps us in the dark

He shows me coloured cards -
a picture all in green. Right away I see
the butterfly balanced on the bike
The optometrist seems impressed
Surprise flickers in both his irises
his hollow cheeks glow red

But I can't make out colours in the dark
I can't see the nose upon my face or peer
in my own ear. I can't see eye to eye with
the man in the moon. I can't see round
corners. I can't see tomorrow. I can't see over the
horizon. I can't see pain or sorrow
Even with a magnifying glass I find no trace
of fairies at the bottom of the garden
I can't focus long on happiness

A blade of grass - fine
A tall ship mast - A 1
Another's point of view - some of the time

The optometrist says my eyes are fine.

Cave Woman Hand
(after a visit to the caves at Pêch-Merle)

As a child I played my games alone
my only friends were Water, Earth and Stone

I loved to dip my hand into soft mud
then press it flat on cold grey stone
I'd smile to see the mark I made -
five fingers, a small palm
held bravely up to halt the march of Time
But Time ignored my child's command -
she called her sidekicks, Wind and Rain;
my handprint soon was gone

Today I heard a guide explain
in France, deep underground
how a woman pressed her hand
against a chilly cavern wall
then on it blew soft ochre paint
through a hollowed reindeer horn

I wonder if she smiled to see
a slender wrist, a flattened palm,
five fingers - fine, feminine, outlined
left behind
for twenty thousand years

I can't begin to understand the distance spanned
by twenty thousand years
Even on the abacus of stars we both have shared
I can't add up that far

But I can recognise the game she played
and smile to see the stencilled print she made:
her pre-historic human hand
her long ago cave woman hand
looks just the same as my hand does today

And childhood doesn't seem so far away.

The Park
A Nursery Rhyme for the Nineties

This is the park where the children play
And this is the glass where you'll cut your knee
Smashed here last night by a bitter youth
(He was smashed too, to tell you the truth).

And this is the frame where the swings should be
But they swung them too high, right over you see
Until they were twirled twelve feet from the ground
And no-one can bother to put them back round
In the park where the childen should play.

This is the chute where the children slide down
It's high so high right up to the sky
But if you should try to get to the top
You'll fall through the bit where the safety rails stop
On the chute where the children fall down.

And this is the spot where the sand-pit should be
But since dogs sniffed it out as a good place to pee
There's just shit in the pit where the soft sand should be.

So this is the park where the children should play
But wise mothers all warn "Kids stay well away!"
From the park where the children should play.

Billy Cans

Away up to the big house
see if she'll boil a kettle
for the billy cans

So ordered I picked up five cans by their wires
trudged to the back door of the house
(tradesman's entrance; I was well-trained in deference)

shyly asked a woman with a peeny
(her good clothes too, and this a working day)
to boil some water for the billy cans

Back with the water and the tea put on the brew
the men made a bench from a skelfy plank
Silently I crouched beside the cans

labels for baked beans, meatballs, pineapple chunks
long since peeled off; curved handles flat
against the burnished tin - the navvy's calabash

A fine lad you've got there
old Billy grunted at my dad
We'll make a worker of him yet

I blushed to the roots of my short-cropped hair
ashamed on two counts -
I was no lad and I aspired

to be a woman with no peeny
dressed Sunday-best on Mondays
sipping tea from fragile china cups

sitting pretty in a winged armchair
watching others sweating at their work

Unfaithful Memory

Squatting by his side I watch my father
sharpen six inch nails. On this side
his left hand turns the handle of the

small machine, the smooth wood cradled snug
between his calloused palm and thumb
Entranced I listen to the rhythmic whirr and hum

soothing as a mother's soft-tongued song
On the other side the click and spin of
metal pin on prehistoric flint. Rasping it

spits electric blue, incandescent white, fluorescent
pink. He quickly checks each silvered point
flicks each sharpened nail into a tin

My father claims my memory's playing tricks -
he never did such work, it seems. Yet
in my head the scene is sharp and clear

and I am left to wonder what it means
when memory flirts so easily with dreams

The Senile Dimension

So sorry, dear
to hear
poor dear,
about
your father's
senile dimension

1 Breathing Space

You are riotously funny
a one-man farce
you clown around
toppling the routine
of all our lives

First off there is
the dressing of you
vest over shirt
socks over shoes
Surrealist in Senility

At tea-time you babble
perched on a flip-top bin
(we really flip our lids at that)
You dollop butter in brown tea
shake sugar on white bread
then down it all   seasoned
with our mirth

You are riotously funny
Laughter gives us breathing space:
all too soon we'll face
the final scene
not of one-man farce
but family tragedy

2 Salting the wound

The baby brings out the best in you
she alone makes contact
in your broken mind

You cosset, cajole, cuddle
like any doting grampa
She giggles, gurgles while
for her you haltingly unmuddle
a few syllables of sense

The baby brings out the best in you
brings smiles to your lined face
rubs salt in the raw wound
where life and death are caught
where only the very young
and the very old
are free to laugh and meet

3 Broken

The Machine is broken
It does not respond
to normal commands
It operates
but erratically

I have phoned
I have phoned

The Repair Man cannot call today

The Machine is definitely broken
It's memory has rewound
It jams on replay replays replays
scenes from childhood days

The machine is losing power
Even its basic functions
cannot be relied upon

I watch it consantly

I am afraid of the Machine
I think it might be dangerous
The children should be warned
Someone should unplug it
But no-one will

I have called the Repair Man
The Repair Man cannot call today

4 Dayroom

Minnie sings sweet as the mina bird
in the jungle of the dayroom
Her yellowed dot eyes dart from chair to chair -
she fears the apes and tigers hiding there

Andy claps the bumbling clowns
they stage to take away his gloom:
he loves the crazy unmatched clothes
the gormless smiles, the pear-drop tears
the cartoon comic frowns
He claps claps claps them
when they tumble down
in the circus of the dayroom

The window rambles on
and on and on
with memories of the War
and the General Strike, and the first TV
and remember wee Aunt Annie
and rides in her flash car
to the captive audience
it reflects upon
in the mystery of the dayroom

Life goes on and on and
makes no sense to you or me
in the hot air of the dayroom

5 Visiting Time

not yet widows, not quite wives
a clockwork army they arrive
wielding lipstick smiles like
tiny blood-red riot shields

They breach the locked ward doors and
dig from bulging shopping bags
today's provisions - sandwiches
home-made cakes, chocolate bars

the old men mumble
the old men stumble
the old men fumble
the old men grumble

And the not yet widows, not quite wives
unwrap with swift efficiency
from tightly-wound clingfilm

this week's slice of love
sandwiched in a fresh-baked sponge
delicately iced with guilt
lightly spiced with sympathy

The food is offered, mauled
by toothless gums, the good wives
bend to wipe the old men's chins, then
feed the fallen crumbs to gape-mouthed bins

The women gather at the locked ward door
display their lipstick smiles, say
firm farewells to men they know
are on their way nowhere

And with their emptied bags
their emptied hearts
the not yet widows, not quite wives
depart

6 No-one cries, not anymore

In the psycho-geriatric ward
he wears slippers
which are not his
he wears trousers, socks
a shirt which belong to
no-one
Not anymore

In the psycho-geriatric ward
his soul is trapped in a cage
even you could not wriggle out of

He wears a smile
which is not his
(not like we knew)
He bears a crown of thorns
inside his head
which should be left on
No-one

And No-one's eyes are closed
No-one's hands are tied with red tape
he claims is not his
he claims he cannot struggle out of

No-one hangs his head and cries
this problem is not his
in the psycho-geriatric ward

In a Paris Supermarket
July 13th, 1989

We were bantering about what to buy - I
planned a Coq-au-Vin to celebrate
the Revolution. You said why not go
the full hog, pig out on a leg of pork
cooked in cream and Calvados and
our trolley was full enough to feed
a Third World Nation when we saw him

He had a loaf of bread pointed
at the check-out girl. She was
counting out the pile of coins
he'd emptied from a purse. You
thought he was seven and I said
nine or ten but underfed

He didn't have enough to buy the bread. But
he waited like a wide-eyed rabbit frozen
in the middle of the road with a bottleneck
of trolleys queuing up to run him down

Two francs more, the girl said really loud
but we were too stressed out, tapping our toes
and tutting, or maybe we were mesmerised by
muzak but no-one made a move and suddenly
the child ran off without the loaf

Let's leave this trolley here, you said,
I'm not hungry anymore and I guess
we're still a hundred years too early
to celebrate the Revolution

The stolen smile

In the tent the women gather
The ten-year old girl with
eyes big and dark as Africa
is led in by her mother

We will make you beautiful
says an old wise woman
and the child tries hard
to smile her smile
which is beautiful

They lay the young brown body
on the cool wood of a table
They tell her they will make
her so desirable
all the men will want her

The women sway and chant
the women sway and chant so loud

the village pigs go squealing off
the birds go squawking high into the sky

And as the weeks go by
the women wonder
at the rawness of her wound
at the redness of her blood

And the girl stares at the children
who are not desirable like her

and she doesn't want to play
and she doesn't want to pee
and she doesn't want her mother

she only wants her smile
and wonders why
the older, wiser women
stole it from her

Not Poverty

(following a speech in which a Tory politician claimed there is no poverty in Britain and criticised claimants for squandering 10% of their allowance on alcohol)

This is not Poverty
says the grey-suited man
slipping off to sip his G&T
(0.01% per day of declared income)

This is not Poverty
says the grey-suited man
feeding the greedy with statistics
they savour over small-talk
swallow whole
regurgitate at will

Poverty is
swollen bellies
on brown skins
dusted with the sands of deserts
far, far away from
our proud Nation's door

And the baby cries
suckling at the Nation's empty breast
and the small child cries
gasping at the dried-up well
of human kindness

But the grey man says
10% of precious little
slugged for cold comfort
means the spirit of compassion
can be plugged back in its bottle

And still the children cry
in the DHSS rooms
Cry for something more
        than begging bowls
        cold comfort
        bland statistics

Cry for the far away brown children
cry for the far away grey men

the men who reassure
Poverty is no more

the country with no name

1

in the country with no name
they lined up all the buts and ifs
they lined up all the whys
they lined the question marks against a wall
and shot each one between the eyes

only the children were left
silently painting a thousand Guernicas
with bloodied fingers

2

lines of makeshift beds in school gymnasiums
lines of staring eyes behind the chickenwire

lines where people hungry for peace
are struck by mortars while they wait for bread

stretch lines on the swollen bellies
of impregnated women

washing lines where the clothes of the newly dead
twitch in the breeze

lines of despair cut deep in the faces
of the dispossessed

demarcation lines
front lines
confrontation lines

enemy lines which ebb and flow
across a blood-soaked map
on a tide of human suffering

so many lines in one small war
and still no-one will draw the line
and say, enough, no more

3

Private Greed relaxes between offensives
dressed as a tree
but for the jackboots
and the blade in his right hand

his left hand cups an apple, he slips
the blade beneath its tight red skin, a
ribbon of red and pink twists from his fist
the white flesh weeps, desire seeps from his lips
a final nick, the skin flicks to his feet

behind him cherry trees hang thick with blossom
the sky is blue, the world is still beautiful

by his feet a machine gun sleeps
like a faithful dog
its muzzle black and warm

Private Greed squints at the fireball
of the sun, then sinks his teeth
deep in the apple's flesh

in the distance a child is wailing
a village is smouldering, Mother Courage
is dragging her cart, her shoulders bent
her feet bloodied and sore

Private Greed spits out
seven glistening pips
grinds his jack-boot heel
hard on the apple core

4

will your people raise monuments in honour
of you who fought your neighbours

will they raise monuments
tall and white against the sky
built from the bones
of your neighbours' children

will your fathers drape your coffins
with your nation's flag

will they drape your coffins
with a blue-veined flag
stitched from the skins
of other men's daughters

will your mothers speak your names with sadness
will the skies weep with the shame of it

will your brothers light a yellow flame
in memory of you who fought and died

will the flame burn forever
will it be a flame of hatred

The Illness

She called herself an artist, drew
disapproving glances. Her
purple feather boa got

up her neighbour's noses
Her tie-died leggings
on the laundry line

gyrated lewdly. Her henna-ed
hair waved like a red rag
at the sacred bull

of their conventions
To top it all her wide-
brimmed hat, sparkling

with hand-sewn sequins set
her neighbours in the shade
They talked behind her back

as long as she was well
within earshot. No-one was
surprised when illness struck

Rumours spread like spores
germinated in the heat of
ignorance. Fear sprouted up

and down the street like hogweed
on a riverbank. She
wasn't long in hospital

Not considering
That first night home the
neighbours popped a message

through her door

human shit

later there were letters
never signed
wishing get well

out of here. After
the funeral a stranger came
On the lawn he piled her papers

paints, half-finished canvases
and set the pyre aflame. He
nailed a *For Sale* sign onto the gate

Later he would write the blurb:
nice house, good neighbourhood,
friendly, clean estate.

PRISONERS SHOULD ONLY WRITE BELOW THIS LINE

The paper's lined. The writing is confined
between its horizontal bars. The pen is like
the ones we got in school. 36 pupils, 36 pens,
36 holes they must be fitted in. Lessons to be
learned. Dates swallowed. Seven-times-seven makes
seven a lucky number. Our Father which art in Heaven,
pencil errors can be erased.

INK IS A SERIOUS MATTER

Mistakes cannot be hidden. The stiff tawse stings
the chastened skin, leaves red stains
on the white sheets of my childhood.

I never fitted. At last they've got me in a hole
cell-hole, hell-hole. My sins will never be forgiven.

Mattress, Desk, Book, Pen
Let me start my life again.

I cannot weep. Visitors are few. Sometimes
the sun creeps through the waffle grill. I
stare until wet claws close my eyes. Sun-dogs
of hell. I cannot sleep. On the wall's a poster

of a kitten. Scratching the dark
I hear it caterwaul.

Ding Dong Bell, Pussy's in the well.
Will they ever?   Sir?

Maybe I'm a Princess in a Fairy Tale. My Father's
in Heaven. He's a King. I lost the Lucky Numbers.
The Black Knight locked me in. The Bad Witch ate
the dates. Blood oozes red ink on white skin.

SINS CANNOT BE ERASED

I am Rapunzel. They cropped my golden hair.
The Sorcerer keeps me here. His white coat
frightens me. I trade him nightmares for a
fistful of rainbows and a magic key - see,
it looks just like a pen - it unlocks my head.

Between the bars on paper wings I can fly free.

NOTE: The tawse is a heavy leather strap used until a few years ago in Scottish schools as
a punishment.

The Coat

It was not that he needed the coat.
But the rich red clay, the faded heather hues
the brooding granite grey, the rippled water blues
all delicately intertwined and woven through
were pleasing to the eye.
Perhaps it were not his to take - but who should care?
It cost him little effort to aquire.

It was not that he coveted the coat.
It was not studded with dazzling diamonds like Africa.
It was not lined with shimmering silks like India.

He found it damp and cold -
and lined its pockets with sheep's wool.
He found it had dark secrets hidden deep
and mined its richest seams of coal.
He used it for his dirty work:
he marred its valleys with industrial stains
he scarred its sunsets with bings, stacks and cranes
till he lost interest and no longer found
it pleased his eye or greased his bank account.

For years he tucked it out of sight except for Hogmanay
when trussed up in tartan he trooped it out
for a laugh and harmless fun - to air it for a day.

He didn't want it anymore
with its awkward threadbare smell of poverty -
he'd give it to some Third World Charity.
But emptying the pockets first
with greedy green-eyed glee he saw
ribbons of black satin pour
with unexpected beauty from
its bleak and chilly north-east shore.

That was it. He wanted it.
He loved its oily black -
he
would not give it back.

Ordinary Joe

Let me show you Ordinary Joe
Ordinary Joe's a dog of war
(once he was your father's twin
once he was your sister's son
once he was the boy next door)

Ordinary Joe's a dog of war
barking mad, ordinary mad
see him howling at the moon
purple, swollen as a bruise
see him snarl and growl and roar

Ordinary Joe's a dog of war
he grows fur beneath his skin
sprouts curled claws on foot and fist
he knows fangs within his jaw
tastes warm blood upon his lips

Ordinary Joe's a dog of war
see him mark the land as his
pissing bullets where he will
shitting death with mortar shells
ever thirsting for the kill

Ordinary Joe runs with the pack
Joe's a lad, he loves to fuck
loves to rut, loves to strut
he fucks bitches when he can
fucks their futures, fucks them up

Let me show you Ordinary Joe
when the killing's done
Ordinary Joe goes limping home
tail tucked low between his legs
bleating, bleating sheepishly
where's the future gone?

Death of a Pacifist

At ten she decided
she would not consume the flesh
of fellow creatures

She sent withering looks
at little boys
who blew up frogs with straws

She worried over prawns; they didn't show
the cuddly qualities of lambs
they didn't have the mournful moaning voice of cows
they didn't have the fragile grace of birds
they only had those black bead eyes
that stared and worried her

She grew into canvas shoes
she boycotted biology
she shunned lucky rabbit's feet
she spurned even the Oxfam furs
she checked every lipstick for a smear
of cruelty; she would not let them claim
they tortured in her name

Her baby blossomed
She rocked him in his crib

And when the fly
the foolish fly
with its germ infested feet
alighted on his sleeping face
she squeezed the blue-black body
between her thumb and finger
and knew she too could be
a murderer

Avalanche

You somersault
frantic starfish of arms and legs
eyes bulge
mouth gulps
you thrash like a dying fish
out or your element
in a tidal wave of snow

The mountain you would conquer
claims you as her own:
she wraps her wedding dress
around you like a winding sheet:
hugs the warm air from your flimsy lungs
binds your limbs with snowy veils
plugs your ears with frosted finger-nails
blinds your eyes with ice-cold tongues

Finally enslaved, your body lies
on the steep slab of her breast
Tiny snowflakes tip-toe softly past
like curious wedding guests. Her kisses
crush against your still warm skin
trickle in a glacier stream
between your parted lips

As darkness wings across her face
your startled eyes decipher
on the deepening sapphire sky
tomorrow's headline in a braille of stars

CLIMBER LOST IN AVALANCHE

The mountain heaves a deep contented sigh

The Bunjee Jumper

falls
opens from a foetal curl
gravity
grabs him by the head

he falls
trailing an umbilical cord
pulsating
pure adrenalin

he rushes
arms stretched wide
like a lover
who's been absent
far too long
he rushes to embrace
the roundness
of the earth

the rope slashes the air
whips him back
towards the skies

gravity reclaims her prize
he dives
arms wide
a crucifix of blood
against the blue
he falls from
heaven to earth

he circles now
north south east west
slows
to a swaying pendulum
hangs
like an exclamation mark
above the park

his hands are crossed
against his breast
his eyes are closed
his heart is thunder
stolen from the gods
caged inside his chest

the tall crane drops

he smells the dampness of the earth
feels the slippery-fingered grass
caress his face

weak-kneed and laughing
stretched to ten feet tall
he swaggers off

Kicking Back

Like a small boy tweaking the thread thin legs
from a trapped crane-fly you snap each finger
from the plastic gloves. Silently you scrub
your hands with medicated soap. You glower
at the gurgling tap. You turn back to the bed
where I still lie.

The baby's dead. No,

not the words you said.   But
are they what you?   You tell the nurse,
the Give Up Smoking poster on the wall, the sink
no heartbeat can be heard inside my womb.

I shiver when you wash me down with
cool concern. You press my belly
just once more, your hand corpse-cold
against my pale, still skin. Interesting,
you murmur to the nurse.

Do I have ears, a brain

Movement? you enquire, off-hand,
Oh yes, I'm sure, there was. I was...
my voice off-key skids off, leaves me
limboed in a nightmare land.

The tap's turned off. I gaze into your
mask. I seek your human face.
Swollen on the bed I lie. I bleed
despair on your detached sterility.

My eyes leak tears, make dark stains
on the paper pillowcase.

No-one cares

The tap begins to drip. The stink
of disinfectant makes me feel quite
sick. White-faced the clock stares
from the pea-green wall. It ticks
and ticks and ticks. I tell you not
to worry, all is well. Inside my womb

my baby fiercly kicks

Anno Wreck Sick

I an anorexic   I mean   I
really think thin   real lean
I mean   I've been carried away to
the point where I've all but
disappeared

Poor virgin, pure maiden I was - oh
they wanted me fed up plump, full, fair oh
so femininely fattened for the
rutting rites - they wanted my sweet flesh to be
some sacrifice on the altarbed of adulthood

Anno Wreck Sick - I could
play around with the hollow sound
play frantic antics with semantics   but
that's not what you want to know   oh no let's
get right down to the nitty, dig to the dying bone
search in my shrinking skull the meaty matter of it

So you want to know why I don't
want to grow oh please think of what it -
sweet sixteen get preened for prodding, fumbling
grunting, mumbling while small child me inside
dies crumbling

Scars will heal
Shrink and heal
Shrink my head
I wanna be dead

Cut off your nose, my ma
always said, to spite, she said,
oh ma, how right, how right

Please don't pin my body, man
lovely living butterfly, please
don't try   I'd rather die

So I'll waste the flesh, ruin
your chances, forestall your advances

Anorexic, that's what I am
happy to be carried off
with a rattling laugh in my skinny throat
to my sweet deathbed.

Deadheading the Rose

1 Check-up

Into the doctor's surgery she floats -
a skirt, a pair of shoes, a blouse, a coat
(this medicine man will know her only as
a well co-ordinated set of clothes)

Perched upon a straight-back chair she
chats and smiles, says as she's there
maybe he should take a look...
The doctor pokes and prods and stares; she

disembodies, hovers in the air. Finally he
sinks back in his seat, scrapes
a blue-veined scrawl
across a pale pink sheet

Against the ticking of the clock
she fastens every button on her coat
tucks his re-assurance in her bag
notes her appointment for a mammograph

2 Mammograph

The wating room is not - it is
the dead end of a corridor, four
chairs on their last legs, an
abandoned *Woman*

and a crumpled paper cup. Waiting
for her turn to be x-rayed, she sees
her hands grow old before her eyes:
brown liver spots spread wide, white

knuckles gnarl, arthritic fingers curl
to yellowed claws. Time telescopes so
every minute counts a passing year. She
wipes her sweating palms dry on her lap

suddenly aware that old age might
elude her grasp. *Next!* Like an omen
of ill-will the small word hovers
in the air. She walks in through

the opened door. *Undress*, a voice commands
She's twisted, tugged by strangers' hands
spineless as a bendy doll. She's soft, pink,
warm, alone she stands in a room of

metal arms and legs as robots' ice
cold faces press against her flesh. She
holds her breath and feels the blood
pulse in her head, and hears the click
the whirr, of unseen cameras

3 Salted Fruit

Outside there is a cutting wind
From the third floor window of the ward
she sees pipe-cleaner people curve
against its blade. Wearily

she sits back on the bed, she turns
the tinny head-set up too loud:
its crack and hiss more welcome than
the Latin words and sterile platitudes

the doctors soothe her with
The angry wind abates, snowflakes
float up past the darkening pane
This is gravity defied: they've

turned her whole world upside down
Her cut breast aches. The gods
have sipped its salted fruit
They liked its fleshy taste

They will be back for more

(Note: a cancer can have a grainy appearance.)

4 Friends

They come in waves
some lapping gently
into the flowered bay
where she's marooned

Others crash in merrily
washing her with smiles
splashing the stiff white sheets
with wet-lipped laughter

They joke. They chat. They laugh. They
dodge the jagged rocks - death/cancer/pain
Social manners silently ordain
these words taboo. They joke

they chat, they laugh. Why
do they find it so hard to accept
the one reality in life is death?
Will it prove fatal if they do?

5 Prep

A votive offering she has been prepared
by maidens in white lace caps. With
them her dark confessions have been shared
Together they have prayed, they have wept

Beneath a pulsing blood-warm shower
her body has been scrubbed and scoured
her tears diluted, will-power sapped
In a long white gown she is now wrapped
beneath a pale blue crown her hair's swept back
around her wrist a bracelet's firmly snapped.

For Saint Agatha, it was not like this
no medicated scrub, no time for tears
only a long veil and an early grave
when Decius, envious of her sex and faith
butchered her breasts with vicious shears

Since sunset they have held her to a fast
no food, no drink, no sleep, no rest
Confined in silence to this bowered room
her eyes have trailed the black hands of the clock

have trawled for shooting stars the velvet dark
(to make a desperate wish upon), have thirsted
for the first rays of the sun, the flickering
of shadows on the wall, the signal

that the strong-armed ones are come. No
make-up now, all gold and silver gone
stripped of talisman and wedding ring, she's
helpless as a tiny babe new-born

Grey shadows brush across her whitened face
She sips the potion from the profferred cup
They bear her to the sacrificial place

6 Beneath the anaesthetic ice

Sinking beneath the anaesthetic ice
under a haloed ring of five full moons
she sees the white-robed high priests circle round
the sacrificial slab she lies upon

she is at the mercy of this masked mandala
she who has no amulet
save the fiery jewels of her eyes

The masked ones voices blur
mantras glide like dark owls on the air

she is at the mercy of these hovering mantras
she, who has no covering
save this paper skin

Unfazed by aphasia she floats
a thankful prayer to Hua T'o

she is at the mercy of his sleeping potion
she, who has no magic of her own

The sacred scalpel shines, the slim wrist bends
red petals cascade from the feathered skies
she sucks through every pore the heady scent
the gods lean forward and eclipse the light

she shuts her eyes
her choice is life
she makes the sacrifice

Note: Hua T'o - Chinese physician, credited with the discovery of anaesthetic. He used powdered hemp in wine.

7 Needles

Here comes the medicine man - she's
his voodoo doll, he holds her
in thrall. On his bed she lies
while silently he eyes the
shining needles on his tray

Here comes the medicine man - in
his hands she's made of clay, he
pierces with the silver of his voice
he punctures with the steel-blue of his eyes
he patches with pink plastic skin, he
punishes with needles sharp and bright

the point being
her body has done wrong

call her Eve
she caused the Fall of Man
Mary Magdalen
she lived in sin
she is Pandora
the most guilty one
she loosed disease upon the world
left hope alone within

Here comes the medicine man
the needle glinting in the light
the point being
her body on its own can't fight
the point being
pushed into her flesh
the poison being
pumped into her blood

the point being hard to see -
they call this healing yet
it gives her pain, it makes her sick
it sucks her strength, it drains her dignity

8 Amazon

Don't put her in purdah. She is
no devil woman who would curse
all those who look her way. She
is no less a woman now, no less

a mother, lover, friend, no less
the person you once knew. Transformed
to warrior Amazon she holds her head up high
she bears her scars with dignity

Don't put her in purdah. The shawl
of sympathy you wrap her in
in time becomes a shroud, dead petals
clasped around a fertile head

She will outgrow the shawl one day
like petals let it fall away
Don't put her in purdah. This woman's
not taboo. View her like a portrait

by Picasso - features might have gone
astray, but the essence of the woman
stays unchanged and true

9 Facing up to it

In the raw light of a new day
she shreds her patient's card
and drops the pieces in the bin
Her wounds are healed, but

worries nag her still - must she live
her life from day to day, from
one check-up appointment to the next
wondering if the cancer's been wiped out

or has it, like a serpent, buried eggs
inside her brain, her spine, her other breast?
But paper tigers lose their power to scare
if only you can look them in the face

and cancer need not be Death's calling card:
a number nine bus or a speeding train
is just as likely now to end life's game

The future's not the time in which she lives
the present's where life's truly at its best
yet while she frets it drifts into the past.

10 Surfacing

She says she has visited the dark
underbelly of the world. She has
wandered in tunnels and caves
where even the walls weep

for the tortured and trapped
Now she is surfacing, she says, like
a swimmer who has almost drowned
who has known the darkness closing in

Don't mind me, she says, if I
dance barefoot in the park at dawn
if I roll naked in a fresh fall of snow
if I make love in the long grass at noon
if I cry at the drop of a hat
and make eyes at the man in the moon

I am drunk, she says. Drunk
on the laughter of friends, drunk
on the song of the stars and the wind

And I am surfacing
from the dark underbelly of the world
surfacing like a swimmer
who has almost drowned

and has known the darkness closing in

Please come round

Please come round tonight. I really want
to see you. But don't be embarrassed when
I ask you to take off your clothes

outside the door. Lift from your head
that unattractive hat - it shades the
tears and laughter in your eyes. Cast off

that coat of twitching anxiety - by
all means leave it worrying at the door
for your safe return. And that stick

you like to carry to beat yourself
to a misery, lose it on the way or
at the very least leave it lying lifeless

on the front porch floor. Please
come round tonight. I want so much
to see you as you really are.

January's child

I find him wedged between Lectures and Meetings
Driving Courses, Deaths, Birthday Greetings,
with flattened hair, a gap-toothed smile
squatting cross-legged on his brief profile:
cheerful, excitable, eager to please, needs
love, stability, security. Neat balance sheet.
Seven years old. Name is Neil. Neil needs a family.

In the home he gobbles Corn Flakes, gets
ticked off for wanting too much sugar, gets
flicked off for wanting too much love. He
stares out at the winter wood, dreams about a
special tree with branches that can hug and hold.

I hope he never sees this morning's paper
where he is reduced from three foot six to
a few column inches, an out-of-focus photograph.
Gawky in t-shirt and shorts, eager to please
the stranger with the fancy camera, too excited
to sit too long at peace, he squints at the lens,
the camera clicks. January's child runs off.

Balance

At sixteen I was metal
you magnet - big attraction for
an iron maiden
I never meddled in mechanics   but
baby did we click   and
was I lovesick stuck
on you

At twenty you were explosive
I an old flame creeping close again
I poured cold water on the science   but
boy o boy we flashed   we fused   we flared
spearing the dark night air
with our illuminating love affair

At thirty you were positive
I was negative
I day, you night
we chased each other's light
round the world, round the clock, round the bend
never quite apart but never could we spend
time to think, to talk, to get it right

But on magic days Mother Moon and Father Sun
would mount the sky together, hang around a while
reflect each others rays of love
make the children point and smile

We were positive we were negative but
with our little additions
I reckon we added up
to a pretty neat equation

One day we'll sit static on a shelf
dusty bookends leaning lazily against
the lifetime's words we've propped between us

The science of it now seems simple
The essence of sweet love boils down
to sitting tight and
finding perfect balance

Still Life

A pomegranate moon sulks in the sky
inside the ward pale shadows flit
in a high-backed throne Miss Evans sits
I'm losing blood, day in, day out
her voice flows fine yet strong
over the flowered duvet
around the Lucozade
behind the slowly rotting bowl of fruit

Across the fading sky a blood-red river flows
against the icy glass cut flowers crystallise
over the window-sill a spider steals
dragging the fuzzied bodies of dead flies

The pomegranate moon climbs higher still
a burnished coin for travellers from this world
to pay the crossing to the other side

A shroud of silence settles on the scene
the shadows draw the curtains on the moon
Miss Evans knows the journey she'll make soon
but calmly reads a life-style magazine

Women who read the bushes and the skies

Are you of travelling folk
who put down restless roots
pushed through strange green shoots
in my town?

Your hair's too long, too black
stretched tight back in a bouncing pony-tail
defying fashion, flicking off the flack
of scaldies' sharp remarks

I've watched you at the shops
ignore the brash displays
which daily hypnotize
your settled city sisters

I've seen you in a lane
pert pixie on a drystane dyke
crumbled to a lowland cairn
reading the daily paper in
the morning's chill sunlight

You read the bushes too -
thick berries you say
a harsh winter in store
Knowingly you eye the cloudless sky
I smile, I say, I'm sure
you're right - of course you are

Still I feel a little bit afraid
of women who read the bushes and the skies
of travelling folk with roots
twined deep in Mother Earth

Heron

he's hunched up on a rock like a
grey-haired hippy, tuned in
to the music of his own heartbeat

he stares across the bay, scans
the grey horizon for the bird
of paradise he hopes one day he'll meet

from time to time he spreads his great wings
wide like an opera-singer's cloak
puffs out his puny chest as if to serenade

the waves, belches a tuneless croak
then hunches up again. he watches others
drifting in, lifting off

he has reasons not to leave
he likes this calm back-water
he couldn't take the cut and thrust

of life out on the mean-cat streets
he's not cut out to be a patio-performer
his scraggy features never could compete

with the ruddy-breasted robin or the dapple-
throated thrush and anyway he's hooked
on fresh caught fish

he flaps his wings, lifts up and off
neck in a swannish curve, toes pointed back
in genteel affectation

slowly he slopes across the strath
on pterodactyl wings
off to his tree-top garret

in the heronry commune
where he'll lie awake all night and gaze
morosely at the grinning moon

Yellowhammer

Aren't you just the bee's knees? Little bird
born sunny-side-up, jaunty as a jockey
in jasmine silks, out of season sunbeam

in my February garden. You're like a budgie
on the run, squeezed through the bars
of a gilded cage, balaclava'd in butter

to ease your escape. Or a tiny tourist
jetted in from Africa or India
still togged out in sunny climate clothes.

Bright as a nugget hammered from the sun
you dive into a day where winter's sucked
the colour from the world. Mr Smiley

with a beak and wings you butter up
to all you see. Finally you speed away
Feathered Angel in a yellow helmet.

The Lighthouse

Stocky little Celt
he teeters like the last skittle
refuses to topple
no matter what life chucks his way

Day and night
his head throbs with the golden glow
of sunlight through malt whisky
Day and night he flashes
more a welcome than a warning

On his rocky outcrop
he pulls himself up short
digs in his solitary heel
holds a dampened finger
to the sky, leans into
the cold unloving wind

last night I stood beneath the stars
(for Italo Calvino)

last night I stood beneath the stars
with the worries of the world cradled
in my arms and watched the full moon
rise. I sucked in with my eyes its

skimmed milk white and just like Alice
when she stole a slug from the forbidden
phial I shrank and shrank and the moon
grew and grew and I forgot it was

a common-or-garden chunk chipped off
the earth and wished I had a green-eyed cat
a pointed hat and an old broomstick to fly
towards its light. By midnight I had shrunk

so small I couldn't hold the weight of all
the worries of the world one heartbeat longer

I let them fall and waited for some me-to-blame
disaster. But there wasn't. Wide-eyed I watched

the moon's great silver ball roll towards tomorrow
It came to rest on a golden thread where earth
and sky are stitched one to the other. There it
gleamed like a giant's plate of eggshell porcelain

then silently it smashed into the dawn and
a white-haired witch with a green-eyed cat and
an old broomstick came racing out as the day turned
red and swept the shattered moon off to its bed

And after staring at the moon all night
watching it rise, watching it fall
I cannot for the life of me recall
what on earth I had to fret about

Homing Instinct

1

They say the men scooped handfuls of the earth
to take aboard the waiting ships
so grieved they were to leave
the land which knew their birth.

They say the women threw themselves
upon the grass and
tore it with their teeth.

2

Mid-life I find myself
mulling over Scotland's map.

Place names sing like Sirens
from its rocky shores.
Sligachan, Fladda Chuain
Loch a' Chairn Bhainn, Suishnish.

Anarchic words where wind
and ocean swell and rush
against a tight-lipped alphabet.

Barbaric words where wild-haired sounds
are trapped and bound behind a net
of longitude and latitude.

I am lured by this ancient tongue
foreign to my ear, familiar to my heart
torn from my throat a century before my birth.

And I am drawn towards the North
as surely as a needle on a compass

**Does time stand still if no-one's there
to wind the clock, to count the days
to tear the pages from the calendar?**

I wade through waist-deep waves of gorse
and taste an unseen ocean on my lips

A path I cannot see
leads me to the skeletal remains
of what was once a croft

I pause beside a rowan
planted by the door
which is not there

I step inside this roof-less, wall-less
scattering of stones, this house and listen

for the scraping of a spade against
the bitter earth, the barking of a dog
out in the yard, the shouts of neighbours
as they gather wrack down by the shore,
a curse, a song, a laugh, a wind-slammed door

I hear the silence of uncounted years

This place is people-less and overgrown
with brambles, gorse and fern
and memories which are not mine

You cannot own the land

The path stops dead
before a barbed-wire fence
a pad-locked gate
a notice nailed into the wood

NO TRESPASSING
NO ACCESS TO THE SHORE
PRIVATELY OWNED ESTATE

Two centuries of rage caged up
inside my heart erupt
two centuries too late.

Is rage the sole inheritance
the dispossessed can claim?

How dare men think a piece of paper
stamped with foreign words and fancy terms
reserves for them (and them alone)
the ownership of sands and rocks and seas
a billion years of fire and flood and ice and
God-alone-knows-what toiled to create?

I climb the gate.

Six Postcards from Rhue Baigh, Ullapool

1

At night the factory ship
sparkles like an octogenerian's
birthday cake

Even the Atlantic winds cannot blow out
its candles

2

Our binoculars pick out painted lines
on the sleeping hull: Cyrillic alphabet
We scan the dark, deserted decks

Can it be the lettering spells out
Marie-Celeste?

3

We search for treasures on the shore.
In the armpit of a rock we find
a rusting aerosol

ΔΕΟΔΟΡΑΗΤ

4

Through the round eye of the telescope
the cormorant's upturned tail
cuts a dash like a shark's fin

His head bobs up
his curved neck question marks
the silver paper sea
Supper squirms in his beak
He dives again, gets a better grip

His head bobs up
His black face grins
and licks its lips

5

They fly in pairs
skimming the water in the bay
scattering the shag-wooled sheep
scaring the scraggy crows

They are the hunters. Are we
the ones they hunt?

The children stare. The youngest
cries. The oldest swears. In the air
we feel the chill of war

We listen to the deafening call
witness the cruel grace and skill
of jets that swoop like birds of prey
of men being trained to maim and kill

6

Stac Polaidh
snaggle-toothed old hag
gnaws the underbelly of the sky
spits out the icy pips
at pewter-faced Loch Lurgainn

Listening to the silence

I am sitting on this sentence
staring across the bay
like a solitary crow
on a barbed wire fence

listening to the silence.

TARANIS POETRY

The Mating of Dinosaurs
by Bill Oliphant
ISBN   1 873899 30 0   £5.99

Ergonomic Work Stations and Spinning Teacans
by Brian Whittingham
ISBN 1 873899 25 4 £4.99

Painting Shadows on the Tilting Horizon
by Emil Rado
ISBN   1 873899 45 9   £3.99

The Elementary Particles
by Gerry Loose
Images by Kate Sweeney McGee
ISBN   1 873899 60 2   £5.99

Transit Visa (N.W.Africa)
by Bobby Christie
ISBN   1 873899 70 X   £5.99

HOW TO ORDER: send direct or teleorder **to**
Taranis Books, 2 Hugh Miller Place, Edinburgh EH3 5JG
Telephone enquiries 031 343 2054

Trade Discount
Single copy orders 20% Two or more copy orders 33.3%